D1541154

Baseball

Marshall Cavendish
Benchmark

This edition first published in 2010 in North America by Marshall Cavendish Benchmark

Marshall Cavendish Benchmark
99 White Plains Road
Tarrytown, NY 10591
www.marshallcavendish.us

Published in 2009 by Evans Publishing Ltd, 2A Portman Mansions, Chiltern St, London WIU 6NR

Editor: Nicola Edwards
Designer: D.R. Ink
All photographs by Wishlist except for p6 Jeff Zelevansky/Stringer/Getty Images;
p7 Rich Pilling/Stringer/MLB Photos via Getty Images; p9 Jim Rogash/Stringer/Getty Images;
p10 Paul Spinelli/Contributor/MLB Photos via Getty Images; p11 Jamie Squire/Getty Images;
p12 Andy Hayt/Getty Images; p16 matooker/iStock; p22 Doug Pensinger/Getty Images;
p23 John Iacono/*Sports Illustrated*/Getty Images; p25 Frederic J. Brown/AFP/Getty Images;
p26 Omar Torres/AFP/Getty Images; p27 Rich Pilling/MLB via Getty Images

Library of Congress Cataloging-in-Publication Data

Gifford, Clive.
 Baseball / by Clive Gifford.
    p. cm. — (Tell me about sports)
 Includes bibliographical references and index.
 Summary: "An introduction to baseball, including techniques, rules, and the training regimen of
professional athletes in the sport"—Provided by publisher.
 ISBN 978-0-7614-4453-4
 1. Baseball—Juvenile literature. I. Title.
 GV867.5.G58 2010
 796.357—dc22
                                    2009009457

The author and publisher would like to thank Logan Kelling, Amy Mobley, Tory Mobley, Aziz Olubaji,
Connie McMillan, Liam Grieveson, Sharon Achia, and Ros Kelling (Coach) for their help in making
this book.

Printed in China.
135642

Contents

Baseball

▲
Jason Bartlett of the Tampa Bay Rays dives to reach home plate. He is tagged out by Philadelphia's Carlos Ruiz. Baseball features many exciting moments like this.

Baseball is an exciting sport that requires skill and strategy. Two teams of nine players have nine **innings** in which to score **runs**. A run is scored when a player reaches **home plate** after touching first, second, and third **base**. The team with the most runs at the end of the game wins. If the teams are tied at the end of nine innings, extra innings are played until a team has won.

In each inning, both teams have a chance at bat. The team that is not batting is in the field playing defense. The fielding team tries to get the offensive team's players out and to stop them from scoring runs.

A team stays at bat until the defense makes three outs. Players are called out if they get three strikes, hit a ball that is caught by a fielder before it touches the ground,

▲ On a baseball field, the pitcher throws from a raised mound 60 feet (18 meters) away from the batter. The pitcher's teammate, the catcher, is behind the batter.

or hit a ball that is fielded and thrown to first base before the runner reaches it. The fielders can also **tag** a runner out by touching him or her with the ball when the runner is not touching a base.

In professional leagues, such as Major League Baseball (MLB) in the United States and Canada, baseball is watched by tens of thousands of fans in stadiums and by millions more on television.

One of the great things about the sport is that a few friends can play a casual game with a bat, ball, and gloves in a park or other open space.

◄

Umpires run a game of baseball. In the highest levels of the sport such as Major League Baseball, a team of umpires is headed by the umpire in chief, or home plate umpire, who stands behind the batter and catcher.

Hitting Home Runs

At the center of baseball game is the duel between the batter and the pitcher. The batter wants to hit the ball into play without getting an out, but the best hit to get is a **home run**. A home run is when the batter hits the ball far enough that he or she is able to run around the bases and score a run.

In baseball parks, most home runs are hit over the **outfield** fence. The batter can jog around the bases. It is much harder to score on a hit that remains in play because the fielders are trying to get the runners out.

▶

This player is swinging powerfully. If the ball bounces and then goes over the fence, it is an automatic double, not a home run.

Home Runs

Babe Ruth hit at least 40 home runs per season in an incredible eleven seasons. He managed 2,217 runs batted in (RBIs) during his career.

In 1997, the Seattle Mariners hit a record 264 home runs in the season. The Texas Rangers almost matched them in 2005, hitting 260.

Lou Gehrig holds the major league record for career grand slams. He hit a total of 23.

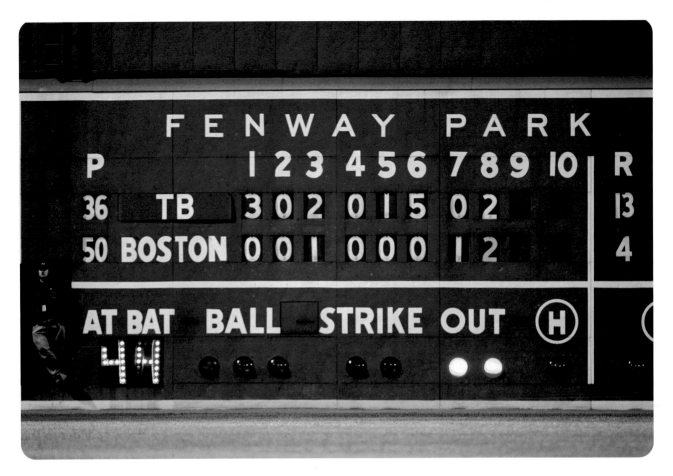

▲ This scoreboard shows that the Tampa Bay Rays (TB) lead the Boston Red Sox by 13 runs to 4 in the eighth inning. The home team always bats in the bottom (second half) of an inning.

Sometimes a batter can score an in-park home run because the fielders make errors. A ball that hits the **foul** pole in midair is also an automatic home run.

Once a batter has hit the ball and heads to first base, he or she becomes a runner. A batter's hit might result in a run if a teammate who is already on base reaches home plate. This is called a run batted in, or RBI, and is recorded as part of the batter's statistics.

When there are runners on first, second, and third, the bases are loaded. If a batter hits a home run in this situation, it is called a grand slam and four runs are scored.

The Baseball Field

Baseball is played on a large, diamond-shaped field. The left and right edges are marked by foul lines that meet at home plate. A ball hit over the foul line is out of play. However, a **fly ball** caught in foul territory still counts as an out. In a stadium, there are also poles in the outfield to help **umpires** determine if a ball is foul or in play.

The **infield** is the diamond made by the three bases and home plate. In the MLB, the bases are 90 feet

▼ This diagram shows the typical field markings and positions of a fielding team.

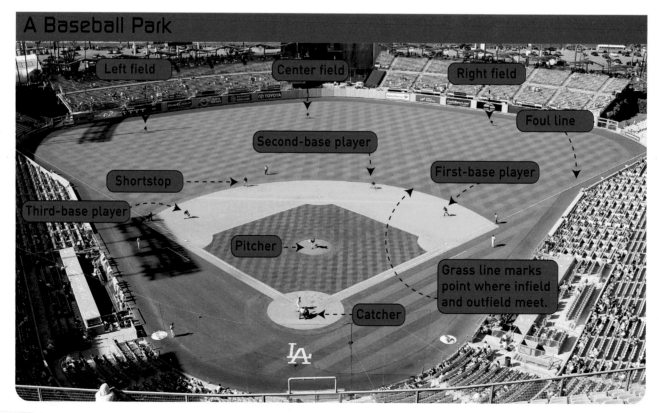

A Baseball Park

Left field

Center field

Right field

Foul line

Second-base player

First-base player

Shortstop

Third-base player

Pitcher

Grass line marks point where infield and outfield meet.

Catcher

(27.4 meters) apart, but smaller diamonds are often used for young players. The pitcher, catcher, shortstop, and the first-, second-, and third-base players are the infielders.

The outfield is the grass-covered area behind the infield that stretches to the park fence or wall. Outfields vary in size. This means it is easier to hit home runs in some parks than in others. The center fielder, right fielder, and left fielder make up the outfield. Some leagues allow two center fielders.

Infields and Outfields

The highest outfield wall in Major League Baseball is at Fenway Park, home of the Boston Red Sox. It is 37 ft (11.3 m) high and is known as the Green Monster.

Minute Maid Park, the home of the Houston Astros, has a flagpole 430 ft (131 m) out in center field! In 2003, the Milwaukee Brewers' Richie Sexson hit the ball into the flagpole!

Most fields also have dugouts or benches where the players sit while watching their teammates at bat. There is usually a bullpen where pitchers warm up and a batting circle where batters can practice swinging.

◄ This fielder wears a typical baseball uniform—a comfortable jersey, a cap, baseball pants, and special shoes called cleats to grip the ground. A large but well-fitting glove is used to catch and field the ball.

► A batter has to stand in one of the two batting boxes on either side of home plate (depending on whether the batter is left- or right-handed). It is important to wear a helmet in case the pitcher throws a wild pitch.

Star Players

The major leagues are home to many of the world's finest players. Members of the thirty MLB teams are professional baseball players because they get paid to play. Top players such as Alex Rodriguez, Ryan Howard, and Manny Ramirez are famous celebrities in the United States.

Despite their wealth and fame, players have to train and work hard. Spring training begins in February and lasts almost two months. Thousands of fans flock to preseason games that are played during this period.

▼

The Los Angeles Dodgers stretch before batting practice. In the middle is star player Manny Ramirez wearing number 99. He has hit over 520 home runs.

▲ First baseman Conor Jackson makes a diving stop. Players need to react quickly to field fast-moving balls.

Players have to be physically fit when the season starts in April. Each team plays a staggering 162 games in the regular season, which runs until October. The winners of each of the MLB's six divisions, plus the two best runners-up, enter the play-offs. Then the top two teams play in the World Series. The team that wins four of the seven championship games wins the World Series.

Fielding

The New York Yankees have won 26 World Series, 16 more than the second-place team, the St. Louis Cardinals.

Injuries and loss of form affect most players at some point. This is why Cal Ripken's record is so remarkable. He began a run of continuous games for the Baltimore Orioles in 1982 and did not miss a game until 1998. He played in an amazing total of 2,632 games!

Alex Rodriguez is one of baseball's top batters with over 550 home runs. In 2007, he signed an eight-year contract with the New York Yankees for $270 million!

Fielding

While it's impressive to see a player make a diving stop or an acrobatic catch, all fielding is important. Fielding **ground balls** or catching fly balls can prevent the other team from scoring runs.

All players, including the pitcher, must be skilled fielders. This only comes with many hours of practice. Many coaches hold fielding practice where the players do drills so they can quickly move to ground balls, judge and catch fly balls, and make strong, accurate throws.

A fielder wears a glove on his or her weaker hand, leaving his or her stronger arm free to throw. Wearing and playing with a glove may feel funny at first.

► This fielder is in the ready position. His legs are spread with his knees bent and his head forward watching the ball and ready to move quickly to field it.

▼ This outfielder reaches up to catch a fly ball. Her eyes watch the ball and her throwing hand is ready to cover the ball once it is in her glove.

▲ This outfielder crouches low to field a ground ball and then springs up quickly. As he does, he takes the ball from his glove, turns, and steps into his throw.

Coaches work with young players to help them get used to the glove and learn how to keep the ball in it.

When a ball goes past the infield, the outfielders must run it down and quickly return it. Outfielders need powerful arms to make strong, accurate throws. When the ball is hit deep into the outfield, one of the infielders will act as a cut-off. This is a player who catches the ball from the outfielder and then throws it to another infielder to try to get a runner out.

The Pitcher

The pitcher is a very important player, but he or she needs a good team in the field. Top pitchers can throw a ball 100 miles (160 kilometers) per hour, but the very best also have great control over the ball's path.

Good pitchers are able to throw different types of **pitches**, such as a fastball and a curveball. Not all pitchers use the same technique. Some release pitches from different arm angles, making it harder for the batter to see the ball.

▼ This baseball pitcher starts his pitching movement by winding up. He then steps forward and unleashes a powerful throw.

◀ Different grips are used to throw different types of pitches. The fastball travels straight through the air at high speed. The curveball spins out of the hand and swerves through the air.

A strike must be over home plate and between the batter's knees and chest, also called the strike zone. If the batter doesn't swing, or swings and misses a pitch in the strike zone, the umpire will call a strike. Three strikes and the batter is out. If the pitch is outside the strike zone, the umpire will call a ball. Four balls and the batter gets to go to first base. This is called a walk.

▼ This box below shows the batter's strike zone. Pitches that travel inside this zone and are not hit are strikes; those outside it are balls. If four balls are pitched to a batter, the batter walks to first base.

Pitchers must also field balls that are hit or **bunted** toward them. They must also keep an eye on the base runners. A pitcher can throw to one of the base players, who will try to tag the runner out before he or she returns to the base.

The Catcher

The catcher crouches close behind home plate and catches the pitches that pass the batter. A good catcher knows a little about each batter so that he or she can suggest what pitch the pitcher should throw. Catchers communicate with the pitcher with hand and finger signals, so the batter doesn't know what to expect. Catchers must also field foul balls and bunts.

Because many pitchers throw very fast, it is important for catchers to wear plenty of protective gear. All catchers wear a helmet with a face guard and throat protector, a chest protector, and leg guards that cover from the knees to the tops of the feet. Boys also wear

▼ This catcher is in a good, balanced stance. He is crouched but ready to spring in any direction. He is keeping his eye on the pitcher.

▼ This catcher is signaling two fingers down to the pitcher. This is their sign to throw a curve ball.

an athletic supporter to protect the groin area. Catchers use a padded mitt, which is larger and more round than a fielder's glove, to catch and field the ball.

A catcher has a tough job. He or she must be alert and agile to catch all sorts of pitches, even if the pitcher throws way off target. Good catchers can leap up and throw out a runner trying to steal second base.

If the ball is hit, the catcher's job isn't over. He or she may have to catch the ball from a fielder and block home plate to tag out a runner who is trying to score.

▲ If a batter hits the ball with the edge of the bat, the ball often pops up into the air. If this happens, the catcher hops up, lifts off his or her mask to get a clear view of the ball, and moves quickly under the ball to catch it.

◄ This catcher throws the ball quickly and accurately to his first baseman. A good throw can get a runner out.

Batting

Before the game starts, the coach decides the batting order. Often a reliable batter will bat first or second, and a powerful hitter will bat fourth, or "cleanup."

Batters stand in one of the two batting boxes depending on whether they are right- or left-handed. Some players are switch hitters and can bat from either side. Batters need to have a good eye, quick reflexes, and great timing to judge whether a pitch is a strike and, if they swing, to connect well with the ball.

If a batter swings and misses the pitch, or hits a foul ball, he or she will receive a strike. If the batter hits a foul ball on the third strike, it is not counted as a strike and he or she stays at bat.

▼ The batter begins with his bat drawn back and his weight on his back foot. He steps toward the pitcher with his front foot and turns his hips and then his shoulders to pull the bat through. He snaps his wrists as he makes contact and finishes his swing before dropping the bat and running to first.

▲ This player is bunting the ball. She has turned to face the pitcher, slid her right hand up the bat, and gently tapped the ball.

▲ A batter grips the bat. The hands are close together and the grip is not too tight.

Sometimes, instead of a long swing, batters try a technique called bunting. A bunt is a gentle hit where the batter brings the bat out front and taps the ball. Coaches often call for bunts when they want a base runner to advance, even if it means the batter is thrown out at first base. This is called a sacrifice bunt.

There are other, less common ways the batter can get to first base beside hitting the ball or receiving a walk. If the batter is hit by a pitch outside the strike zone, he or she advances to first. If the batter standing in the batting box swings at a pitch and the bat touches the catcher, the umpire calls catcher interference and the batter goes to first base.

Infielders

Apart from the pitcher and the catcher, there are four infielders: the first-, second-, and third-base players, and the shortstop. All the infielders must stay alert so they can react quickly when the batter hits the ball.

The easiest way for an infielder to make an out is to throw the ball to a base player before the runner reaches that base. They can only do this when the runner is forced to run. There can only be one runner on each base at a time, so when there is a runner on the base behind you, you must run to the next base.

▼ Darwin Barney leans to catch a throw as runner Mike Cavasinni dives into second base. Infielders need quick reactions to catch, throw, and tag out runners.

An infielder with the ball may also tag a runner who is not on base. You must tag a runner if he or she is not forced to run. When runners slide into a base, the base player should stand in between the runner and the base and hold the ball close to the ground to tag the runner.

Alert players with good fielding skills can sometimes turn a double play, where two outs are made on one play. A triple play is when the defense makes all three outs on one play. It is very rare.

Plays

Cleveland's Asdrubal Cabrera managed to make a triple play all by himself against the Toronto Blue Jays in 2008. He dove and caught the ball, stepped on a base to make a second out, and then tagged out a third player. It was the fourteenth-ever unassisted triple play in Major League Baseball history.

In 2005, the St. Louis Cardinals' first baseman, Albert Pujols, made 175 double plays in the season. This was the most by a major league player in 39 years.

▼ Jason Bartlett of the Tampa Bay Rays dives for home plate but is tagged out by the Philadelphia Phillies catcher, Carlos Ruiz.

Running and Stealing

As soon as a batter hits the ball into play, he or she must start running as fast as possible to safely reach first base. Runners aim to touch the closest edge of the base with their foot before they are thrown out.

Runners are allowed to run past first base into foul territory as long as they touch the base. However, runners cannot overrun second or third base. If they do, they can be tagged out. This is one reason many players slide if it is a close play. When runners try to advance two or more bases on one hit, they usually run in a curve and touch the inside of each base as they sprint hard toward the next.

▼ This runner slides into second base. His front foot skims the ground and he keeps his hands up to avoid injury.

A runner can steal a base when the pitcher pitches the ball. To successfully steal, a runner must have cunning, good timing, and explosive speed. Runners have to be careful. If they leave too early, the pitcher might throw them out. This is called a pickoff. If they leave too late, the catcher might throw them out.

Successful Steals

Rickey Henderson is the all-time leader in Major League Baseball for stolen bases. He has stolen a total of 1,406 bases.

In 2007, the Seattle Mariners' Ichiro Suzuki completed his forty-fifth steal in a row—a record in Major League Baseball.

▼ Hiroyuki Nakajima played on Japan's 2008 Olympic team. Here, he sprints to steal second base as the pitcher makes his pitch.

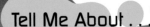

The World of Baseball

Baseball started in the United States, but it has become a popular sport in many countries. Major League Baseball, which has both U.S. and Canadian teams, is the strongest and most popular competition.

The MLB is divided into two leagues: the National League (NL) and the American League (AL). There are also lots of minor league teams in the United States. Players on these teams are paid, but many of them hope to move up to the majors.

Outside of North America, baseball is played in more than 100 countries. Japan was the first Asian country to have professional leagues, though many others do now.

▼ Cuba's Norberto Gonzalez pitches the ball during the final game at the 2008 Olympics. Cuba lost to South Korea 3–2.

▲ Eric Bruntlett slides into home plate to score the winning run in the third game of the 2008 World Series. Bruntlett's team, the Philadelphia Phillies, won the series four games to one.

Baseball has been played in Cuba since the 1870s. It spread to other Caribbean countries, including Puerto Rico and the Dominican Republic, as well as to Central and South America. More than 20 percent of MLB players are from Caribbean or Latin American countries.

There are many national baseball competitions. In Europe, a championship is held every two years. The Netherlands beat Great Britain for the title in 2007. The World Baseball Classic, sponsored by the MLB, features 16 teams from around the world. Japan won the first competition in 2006.

Major Competitions

In 2004 the Boston Red Sox swept the World Series in four games, beating the St. Louis Cardinals. It was exciting because the Red Sox had not won a championship in 86 years!

The first MLB game to be played outside of Canada or the United States occurred in 1996 in Monterrey, Mexico. Since then, MLB games have been played in Puerto Rico and Japan.

Where Next?

These websites and books will help you to find out more about baseball.

Websites

http://www.mlb.com/mlb/kids
The kids' section of the Major League Baseball website has games, interviews with players, and lots of other news and features.

http://www.sikids.com/baseball/mlb
Sports Illustrated's website for kids has a section that covers the MLB, including game schedules, statistics, and news.

http://www.ducksters.com/sports/baseball.php
This site offers a clear guide to basic baseball rules, player positions, and strategies. It also has a glossary of baseball words.

http://www.howbaseballworks.com
A guide to Major League Baseball that explains all about the game, from player statistics to types of pitches to the World Series.

Books

Karapetkova, Holly. *Baseball*. Vero Beach, FL: Rourke Publishing, 2009.

Kennedy, Mike. *Baseball*. New York: Children's Press, 2002.

Baseball Words

bases The four corners of a baseball infield: first base, second base, third base, and home plate. Runners must touch each base to score a run.

bunt A batting technique in which the batter holds the bat out and gently taps the ball into play.

fly ball A baseball hit into the air.

foul When the ball is outside the field of play.

ground ball A batted baseball that rolls along the ground.

home plate The base where the batter stands when up at bat. Runners must touch home plate to score a run.

home run When a batter hits the ball far, usually over the fence, and is able to score a run on his or her hit.

infield The diamond-shaped part of the playing field that includes the bases and pitching mound.

inning The part of a baseball game in which both teams get a chance to bat. Each game has nine innings.

outfield The part of the playing field that is beyond the infield.

pitch A throw made by the pitcher to the catcher that the batter may try to hit.

run A score made by a player who advances safely around the three bases and touches home plate.

tag When a base runner is touched with the ball by a fielder. If the runner is not standing on a base, he or she is out.

umpires The officials who run a game of baseball. They call strikes, decide if a ball is foul, and make sure the rules are followed.

Index

Numbers in **bold** refer to pictures.